CONTENTS

MYTHICAL FANTASY BEASTS!

Myths and legends are filled with friendly beasts such as unicorns or griffins. However, in many stories, heroes faced harpies, minotaurs and other deadly monsters. What would these mythical creatures be like if they were real? What would they eat? How would they behave? Let's find out!

> **myth** story from ancient times; myths often tried to explain natural events

Fact: Ancient people believed sea serpents, griffins and other mythical beasts were real living creatures.

CERBERUS

Size: 2 to 2.1 metres (6.5 to 7 ft) tall

Home: rocky plains and lava fields

Diet: none, it does not eat

Lifespan: unknown

Appearance: Cerberus appears as a huge three-headed dog. Its feet are tipped with sharp claws. Its mouths are full of grinding teeth. Its eyes glow with burning fire.

Underworld place under the earth where ancient people believed the spirits of the dead went

lair hideout used by wicked people to keep their activities secret

Behaviour: Cerberus is a cruel spirit that was given a physical form. A wicked wizard probably raised it from the **Underworld**. It spends most of its time guarding its master's secret **lair**. The beast can belch out balls of fire to burn intruders.

CHIMERAS

Size: 2 metres (6.5 ft) tall, up to 4.6 metres (15 ft) long
Home: dry caves in hilly areas
Diet: deer, sheep, wild pigs, rabbits, sometimes plants
Lifespan: unknown

Appearance: Most chimeras have the heads of a lion and a goat. A few also have a dragon's head. A large, poisonous snake forms a chimera's tail. Their front feet resemble dragon's claws. Their hind feet are goat-like hooves.

Behaviour: Chimeras are beasts created by wicked gods or wizards. They are completely loyal to their creators. They obey orders without question. Chimeras with dragon heads sometimes enjoy attacking villages and collecting treasure.

GORGONS

Size: 1.5 to 1.7 metres (5 to 5.5 ft) tall
Home: caves and ruined castles by the sea
Diet: rats, rabbits, frogs, fish, birds
Lifespan: unknown

Appearance: Most gorgons have scaly green skin. They have sharp fangs and a forked tongue. A gorgon's upper body looks like a human woman. Instead of hair, gorgons have a nest of squirming snakes on their heads.

Behaviour: Gorgons were once beautiful women who were cursed by the gods. They live alone, away from people. Gorgons use powerful magic to defend their homes. One look from a gorgon's glowing eyes can turn intruders into solid stone.

GRIFFINS

Size: 2.6 to 3 metres (8.5 to 10 ft) long;
wingspans up to 7.6 metres (25 ft)

Home: dry caves in grassy hills

Diet: rabbits, deer, sheep, camels, buffalo

Lifespan: 35 to 50 years

Appearance: Griffins have the large head, wings and **talons** of an eagle. Their lower bodies have the powerful legs and sharp claws of a lion. They are covered with a mix of golden hair and feathers.

talon long, sharp claw

Behaviour: Griffins usually live alone. They spend a lot of time flying and hunting for food. Griffins have incredible eyesight. They can spot prey up to 5 kilometres (3 miles) away. Some griffins are friendly and will help people who respect them.

Harpies

Size: 1.2 to 1.4 metres (4 to 4.5 ft) tall;
wingspans up to 2.7 metres (9 ft)

Home: rocky cliffs and small caves near the sea

Diet: fish, crabs, seals, human sailors

Lifespan: about 40 years

Appearance: Harpies have the bodies of vultures. They have strong wings and feet tipped with sharp talons. Their heads appear as monstrous women. They have yellow eyes, greasy hair and rotting teeth.

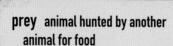

prey animal hunted by another
animal for food

Behaviour: Harpies never bathe. They reek from the bits of rotting flesh stuck to their filthy bodies. Harpies' favourite **prey** is human sailors. They use magical singing to cloud sailors' minds. The music draws sailors close to shore so harpies can attack.

KRAKENS

Size: more than 107 metres (350 ft) long
Home: large caves on the ocean floor
Diet: fish, sharks, whales, human sailors
Lifespan: unknown

Appearance: Krakens look like gigantic squid or octopuses. They have tough, rubbery skin and ten **tentacles**. Krakens have wide mouths filled with sword-like teeth. Their large, 1.8 metre- (3 mile-) wide eyes give them excellent vision.

tentacle long, arm-like body part some animals use to move, touch or grab things

Behaviour: Krakens enjoy fighting ships and the taste of human flesh. A kraken first crushes a ship in its huge tentacles. It then stuffs the doomed sailors into its mouth. It is thought that krakens age very slowly. They may live for more than 1,000 years.

MINOTAURS

Size: 2.3 to 2.4 metres (7.5 to 8 ft) tall

Home: maze-like networks of underground caves and tunnels

Diet: sheep, pigs, goats, goblins, humans

Lifespan: up to 300 years

Appearance: Minotaurs have legs and heads like a bull's. Their arms and **torsos** resemble a human's. They are covered in shaggy hair and have yellow eyes. They attack enemies and prey with sharp, deadly horns and claws.

torso part of the body between the neck and waist, not including the arms

Behaviour: Minotaurs live alone in dark caves and tunnels. They have excellent vision and are fearsome hunters. They spend most of their time prowling for their next meal. Minotaurs have an amazing sense of direction. They never get lost in their dark, maze-like homes.

Pegasi

Size: 2.6 to 3 metres (8.5 to 10 ft) long;
wingspan up to 7.6 metres (25 ft)

Home: forests and grassy plains

Diet: grass, oats, apples, carrots, beets

Lifespan: 50 to 70 years

Appearance: Pegasi have strong horse-like bodies with powerful wings. They can fly up to 80 kilometres (50 miles) per hour. They are usually white or light grey in colour.

tame train a creature to live with and be useful to people

Behaviour: Pegasi enjoy their freedom. They are not easily **tamed**. They are good judges of character. They sometimes become friends with people who show them respect and kindness. Pegasi do not tolerate evil. They react violently towards wicked people.

Phoenixes

Size: 3 to 3.7 metres (10 to 12 ft) long;
wingspans up to 9 metres (30 ft)

Home: rocky cliffs in mountain regions

Diet: rabbits, sheep, goats, deer, warthogs

Lifespan: unknown

Appearance: Phoenixes are also called firebirds. They are covered in bright red feathers that glow with fire when they become angry. Phoenixes are strong enough to carry away an adult elephant.

Behaviour: Phoenixes usually live far from humans. They are noble creatures. They sometimes help wise wizards fight the forces of evil. When a phoenix reaches the end of its life, it bursts into flame. Then a newborn phoenix chick appears in the ashes.

Sea Serpents

Size: 46 to 61 metres (150 to 200 ft) long
Home: warm oceans
Diet: fish, seals, squid, whales, human sailors
Lifespan: up to 500 years

Appearance: Also known as sea dragons, sea serpents have giant snake-like bodies covered in tough scales. They often have dragon-like heads and mouths filled with deadly teeth. Some also have large fins that look like dragon wings.

Behaviour: Sea serpents spend most of their time hunting for prey. They will sometimes attack human ships. These giant creatures first coil their bodies around the ships to crush them. They then eat the doomed human sailors.

UNICORNS

Size: 2.6 to 3 metres (8.5 to 10 ft) long
Home: grassy clearings in large forests
Diet: grass, ferns, berries, other leafy plants
Lifespan: more than 1,000 years

Appearance: Unicorns look similar to large white horses. These mythical creatures have bright blue or violet eyes. Their main feature is the magical **ivory** horn that grows from their heads. Evil wizards sometimes create powerful magic wands using unicorn horns.

> **ivory** hard, creamy-white material that makes up an animal's tusks or horns

Behaviour: Unicorns are fierce protectors of the forest. They will quickly attack any wicked creature in the forest. Unicorns avoid humans. They are friendly with elves, fairies and other magical people.

Creature quiz

1. You should never look into a gorgon's eyes because:

    A) you could lose your mind.

    B) you could be turned to stone.

    C) it's a sign of disrespect.

2. Unicorn horns are sometimes used to make:

    A) jewellery.

    B) small sculptures.

    C) powerful magic wands.

3. Which group of creatures may be friendly towards humans?

    A) griffins, pegasi and phoenixes

    B) harpies, minotaurs and unicorns

    C) Cerberus, griffins and krakens

4. When a phoenix reaches the end of its life, it:

    A) flies across the ocean to its final resting place.

    B) bursts into flames and is reborn from the ashes.

    C) vanishes in a flash of light.

5. To trap their prey, harpies will often:

    A) use magic to appear as beautiful women.

    B) set up a large table full of food.

    C) sing magical songs to cloud sailors' minds.

6. A chimera has the body parts of which creatures?

   A) a horse, a lion and an eagle

   B) a lion, a goat, a dragon and a serpent

   C) a human, a vulture and a bull

7. A Pegasus may help someone who:

   A) shows it kindness and respect.

   B) feeds it apples.

   C) is a magic user.

8. A minotaur never gets lost in its maze-like home because it:

   A) has excellent eyesight.

   B) has an excellent sense of direction.

   C) both A and B.

9. Cerberus looks like a huge three-headed dog. However, it is really:

   A) a cruel spirit from the Underworld.

   B) a monster created by a wicked wizard.

   C) a person under an evil curse.

10. Which of the following is a favourite food for both sea serpents and krakens?

   A) seals

   B) human sailors

   C) sharks

See page 31 for quiz answers.

29

Glossary

ivory   hard, creamy-white material that makes up an animal's tusks or horns

lair   hideout used by wicked people to keep their activities secret

myth   story from ancient times; myths often tried to explain natural events

prey   animal hunted by another animal for food

talon   long, sharp claw

tame   train a creature to live with and be useful to people

tentacle   long, arm-like body part some animals use to move, touch or grab things

torso   part of the body between the neck and waist, not including the arms

Underworld   place under the earth where ancient people believed the spirits of the dead went

Find out more

Books

How to Draw Fantasy Creatures, Paul Bryn Davies and Jim McCarthy (Search Press, 2015)

Perseus and Medusa (Ancient Myths), Blake Hoena (Raintree, 2010)

Quiz answers:

1:B, 2:C, 3:A, 4:B, 5:C, 6:B, 7:A, 8:C, 9:A, 10:B

Websites

www.dkfindout.com/uk/history/ancient-greece/pegasus
Learn about Pegasus from Greek myths.

greece.mrdonn.org/greekgods/monsters.html
Find out more about Greek myths.

Index